SIX KEY STEPS TO UNLOCKING A HEALTHY AND PRODUCTIVE RELATIONSHIP

Dinelly Holder, Ph.D.

Copyright © 2022 Dinelly Holder

All rights reserved.

Content in this book is not intended in any way to be a substitute for face-to-face, professional, medical, psychiatric, psychological, or behavioral health care advice and should not be relied on for medical, psychiatric, psychological, or behavioral health diagnosis or treatment.

Higher Pathways Publishing

ISBN 979-8-9871965-7-1

Editing by KarolynEditsBooks.com

Reach the author at:

https://www.higherlifepathways.com/

https://www.higherlifepathways.com/blog

Email: drholder@higherlifepathways.com

Instagram: @drholder_hlp

Twitter: @drholder_hlp

Facebook: Higher Life Pathways - Dr. Holder

Postal: 1800 Diagonal Road, Suite 600

      Alexandria, VA 22314

I want to thank my parents for showing me the importance of commitment through their forty years of marriage.

I want to thank my spouse and siblings for their love, support, and awesome encouragement in all my endeavors, especially in writing this book.

TABLE OF CONTENTS

INTRODUCTION	1
CHAPTER 1 | KNOW THY SELF FIRST	5
CHAPTER 2 | HEALTHY VS UNHEALTHY MARRIAGE RELATIONSHIPS	9
Healthy Marriage Relationships	9
Unhealthy Marriage Relationships	11
CHAPTER 3 | ASSESSMENT OF MARITAL RELATIONSHIP	15
CHAPTER 4 | MARRIAGE BREAKERS	21
Marriage Breaker Attributes	22
Marriage Breaker Categories	24
CHAPTER 5 | MARRIAGE BUILDERS	29
Marriage Builder Attributes	30
Marriage Builder Categories	32
CHAPTER 6 | RELATIONSHIP SECURITY SYSTEM	39
Key RSS Elements	40
RSS Threats	40
CONCLUSION	43

INTRODUCTION

Do you want to experience an "accidental" divorce? Probably not. But if reaching the inner parts of your partner to reconnect and enjoy healthy communication in your marriage relationship is difficult, that is likely where you're headed.

In marriages, couples are often in pain and anguish trying to figure out the reasons for the tumultuous environment that they are experiencing with their partner. When couples recite their vows and say "I do" at the beginning of their marriage journey, they are not envisioning a future in which they think of their partner as an enemy or someone who is not looking out for their best interests. When couples enter a marriage union, they are usually thinking the best of their partner. When there is fighting, thoughts of leaving, fear, and anxiety while speaking to your partner, you may wonder how your relationship entered this realm of chaos.

How life-changing would it be to feel safe again with your partner? How valuable would it be to feel protected and loved by your partner? And how good would it be to feel secure in your marriage relationship? When you are in a happy and joyous marital union, you will feel that you have support, that your partner is your ally, and that you can do anything because you have a forever cheerleader on your team who will be there for you, no matter how terrible life's circumstances may become.

In this book, you will be shown the steps to take and strategies to apply to receive relationship relief, pleasure from your relationship again, and an understanding of how to maintain continuous harmony and peace throughout your relationship, even during times of conflict.

I wrote this book because I have a heart for couples and marriages. I enjoy seeing marriages succeed. When marriages succeed, families succeed; when families succeed, communities succeed; when communities succeed, the general population works better to improve the atmosphere and environment within the social and psychological mindsets of humanity. When your marriage succeeds and when you produce or have guardianship of children that succeed, your successful marriage relationship plays a small part in a larger impact on the overall relational health of the world.

I have been counseling couples for over eighteen years, and the results have been life changing. Countless couples have achieved relationship goals and gained an improved understanding of how to be effective and productive in their marriage journey toward continued happiness and joy within their relationship. After earning my doctoral degree focused on studying conflict styles and strategies in long-term marital relationships, I have counseled a multitude of couples to reaching excellent relationship outcomes. I have seen remarkable results in the lives of married couples who have practiced the strategies described in this book.

My goal throughout this book is to help guide you to be an effective, transformative change-agent within your own marriage and gain peace, success, and satisfaction in your overall life and relationship.

The first steps to accomplishing this goal involve understanding who you are to yourself, who you are in your relationship, and the reasons why you behave the way that you do in the relationship to produce either positive or negative results.

CHAPTER 1
KNOW THY SELF FIRST

Evaluating yourself is important so that you are aware of how you appear and present yourself in the relationship. When you become familiar with your strengths and weaknesses, the focus is placed on you instead of your partner and will help clarify your needs and wants in the relationship. Ask yourself:

- When it comes to being good and positive to yourself, how do you show up for yourself in your life?

- Are you kind to yourself? How do you support and care for yourself?

- Are you gentle with yourself? How are you merciful and lenient with yourself?

- Do you practice self-control? How do you manage your emotions and actions, especially in negative situations?

- Are you faithful to yourself? How do you remain loyal to a specific value or purpose?

- Are you patient with yourself? How do you forgive yourself when you make mistakes? What do you say to yourself when you make mistakes? Are you critical or a positive self-promoter?

- Do you love yourself? Do you enjoy spending time alone? Are you able to practice self-care?

- Do you have joy within your personal life? Are you pleased and happy with yourself?

- Are you at peace with yourself and your decisions? Are you in a constant space of security and calmness? Can you exist by and within yourself in harmony?

If your answer to any of the self-assessment questions is "no," those questions must be addressed to have a healthy relationship with yourself. If you do not treat *yourself* well, by default, you will also treat your relationship partner in an unhealthy manner.

If you are not uplifting yourself, by default, you will not be able to support your partner in a healthy manner. How can you truly be present for your partner in a relationship when you are not present for yourself?

If you are not good to yourself on a regular basis, how can you start? What steps can you take to begin practicing positivity with yourself?

Answering these questions will help you to address aspects of your life that might be lacking that may potentially put a strain on the relationship with your partner. Honesty with yourself during this self-assessment may show you the areas you need to individually build on to be a better partner for your spouse in your marital relationship.

CHAPTER 2
HEALTHY VS UNHEALTHY MARRIAGE RELATIONSHIPS

Is your marital relationship healthy or unhealthy? Defining a healthy marriage relationship means gaining awareness of the healthy and unhealthy parts of your own marriage. Finding a solution to problems within your marriage and achieving lasting and effective relationship results requires finding and understanding the problems.

Healthy Marriage Relationships

Which elements build a healthy marriage? A healthy marriage consists of couples working together for the satisfaction and success of the relationship. When working together, communication is a key element because couples must be willing to speak to each other for continuing clarity and understanding. They must be willing to agree with each other when contemplating decisions that affect their relationship. Couples must also be willing to handle conflicts to prevent misunderstandings or issues in the future. Couples must be willing to support each other and keep their focus on helping each other in times of both distress and harmony. In addition, couples must be willing to develop and maintain trust in each other to maintain a lasting relationship.

In a marriage, stressors can enter the relationship for a variety of reasons. However, when couples invest in adopting different ways of handling issues, it can lead to a successful marriage relationship. A willingness to work on improving their emotional connection in the relationship increases the value and respect in the relationship. Spouses who are emotionally supportive can expect to see positive outcomes in conflict resolution and communication in the relationship.

The goal of a healthy and long-term marriage is for both individuals to treat each other in a harmonious and respectful way, which can lead to enhanced communication and increased peace in the relationship's atmosphere and environment.

Having a supportive network and resources can improve the health and strength of a marriage relationship. Supportive networks and resources can include childcare from family and friends, marriage-centered seminars, retreats, and professional counseling. Taking advantage of these networks and resources when necessary certainly improves marital longevity and satisfaction. Also, sharing in activities together, such as family vacations, romantic getaways, and self-care activities that increase both partners' happiness and contentment improves the health of the marital relationship.

Unhealthy Marriage Relationships

Which elements can break down a marriage? What makes a marriage unhealthy?

A variety of dynamics can erode a marriage relationship. For example, infidelity, financial issues, communication issues, etc. However, before those dynamics evolve, emotional factors initiate the breakdown. The premise of the phrase "cause and effect" is that an effect will follow a cause. In this case, infidelity is an example of an effect. Its cause could be emotional factors, such as unresolved hurt, anger, disappointment, resentment, or bitterness. When these emotional factors remain unresolved for a long period of time, the effect is almost always an end to the marriage relationship, culminating in divorce.

When partners hurt each other and show no consideration for the emotional or psychological damage done to the injured partner, emotions rise to the next level, which is anger. Anger is a secondary emotion. Hurt is always the first emotion. When hurt turns to anger and the injured partner continues to ignore and avoid their anger, it can turn into discontentment because they may begin to feel disillusioned and sad that their partner does not care about their emotional well-being. As the feelings of hurt, anger, and discontentment continue to fester within the injured partner, resentment begins to grow within their heart. Resentment can remain within the heart and mind of the injured partner for months or even years. Eventually, feelings of resentment will turn into bitterness, causing an individual to view their partner as their enemy based on how they have been hurt by them in the past. Releasing the pain and hurt of what your partner has said or done to you in the past becomes very difficult. Ultimately, the increasing sequence of unresolved emotions can lead to the end of a marriage relationship.

Defining a healthy and unhealthy marital relationship may clarify the factors that may need to be adjusted in your own union with your spouse. Healthy relationships strive to focus on what is working versus what is not working in the relationship. Unhealthy relationships focus on the negative factors, regardless of the positive factors. Each day, married couples have the opportunity to choose whether their mindset will focus on the negative or the positive factors of their relationship. What are you choosing to believe about your spouse and relationship on a daily basis?

CHAPTER 3
ASSESSMENT OF MARITAL RELATIONSHIP

In a marital relationship, honesty is always the best policy! This chapter will help you determine where your current relationship stands and how you can create a path for writing a successful relationship story with your partner.

Jot down your answers to each of these questions:

1. What is the current state of your marital relationship?
   Great [ ]   Good [ ]   Okay [ ]   Bad [ ]

2. Describe the perfect relationship. What is your relationship paradise?

3. When you met your partner and thought about the future of the relationship, what did you imagine? Did you imagine growing older together, having children, traveling the world together, creating a legacy, working together, and going on new adventures together?

4. In what area of the relationship do you think you need the most help with?

5. In relationships, some problematic areas require assistance to improve the relationship bond. What are a couple of those areas in your relationship?

6. In what area of the relationship do you think you need the least help with?

7. What has been working for your relationship? What are a couple of areas that your relationship excels in?

8. Have you sought relationship help in the past? For example, books, couples retreats, couples counseling, family assistance, religious assistance, social media, internet, etc. If you have, please list what you have tried.

9. Why didn't the previous strategies work for your relationship? Why do you feel past relationship help didn't necessarily work for your relationship?

10. Are you ready to do the internal and external work required to create your perfect relationship? This would include trying many of the strategies presented in this book.

    Yes! [ ]   No [ ]   Unsure [ ]

11. What makes you ready to change or adjust your behavior to achieve the perfect result? How do you know whether you are ready to do whatever it will take to make your relationship work?

12. What obstacles would block you from obtaining your perfect relationship?

13. How does your relationship benefit you?

14. What are some examples of your continuous positive contributions to improving your relationship?

15. How do you believe your partner experiences *you* in the marriage relationship? What is your partner's perception of you as a person and as a partner in the relationship? Is there a difference between the two?

Honestly completing your relationship assessment may show you that changes within yourself and in the relationship may need to be made and that you may need to adjust to increase the joy and harmony within your relationship. More importantly, this honesty with yourself about your relationship will also highlight the multitude of positive possibilities available.

CHAPTER 4

MARRIAGE BREAKERS

In this chapter, you'll learn what a marriage breaker is, how it affects a relationship, and whether you are dealing with any in your relationship.

The goal of this book is to find the solutions to any issues you're experiencing in your marriage relationship and regain peace and satisfaction. Now that you've assessed your marriage relationship, you need to know how your specific issues arose so that you can do something about them and keep them from reoccurring. When a relationship is in trouble or failing, and one or both partners are ready to leave the marriage relationship, marriage breakers are usually the culprits responsible for the ending of the relationship.

What is a marriage breaker? A breaker is an action that tears apart, demolishes, downgrades, creates obstacles, and always focuses on the problem instead of the solution. During conflict in a relationship, harsh and critical words may be used to cut down your partner, hurt their feelings, or cause them to feel disrespected. Words can inflict pain upon your partner and tear away emotional closeness. Words or actions may consistently and intentionally harm your partner, thereby increasing the distance between the two of you, resulting in separation or worse, divorce.

Marriage Breaker Attributes

The following attributes are marriage breakers that work against your relationship and contribute to its destruction. The related questions will assess where you are presently in your relationship.

- Envy, jealousy – Do you have feelings of discontent aroused by your partner's life or other couples' lives?

- Arrogance – Do you frequently glorify yourself and brag about accomplishments? Do you create a domineering or oppressive environment in your household? Does your partner?

- Dishonor – Do you shame or disgrace your partner to their face, behind their back, or in front of friends and family?

- Selfishness – Do you lack consideration for your partner? Are you concerned solely with your own personal profit or pleasure in the relationship? Is your partner?

- Anger – Do you consistently express displeasure, annoyance, or hostility in your relationship through verbal, emotional, or physical actions? Does your partner?

- Resentment – Do you practice an unwillingness to forgive your partner for hurting you, even if they apologize? Does your partner practice this behavior toward you?

- Dishonesty – Do you tend to mislead your partner through gaslighting or outright lying? Does your partner practice this behavior toward you?

- Obnoxiousness – Are you extremely unpleasant for your partner to be around, especially during conflict? Do you habitually hurt your partner, whether intentional or not? Do you believe that your partner treats you in this manner?

- Tendency to gossip – Do you relay private and personal information about your partner and relationship to family and friends? Does your partner participate in this behavior toward you?

Marriage Breaker Categories

Marriage breakers can be divided into three categories.

- Action breakers

    Dishonesty
    Dishonor
    Obnoxiousness

Action breakers consist of behaviors and activities that demonstrate a continual harmful and toxic path toward the destruction of a particular relationship. Dishonesty, dishonor, and obnoxiousness directly contribute to the dismantling of a relationship.

When you are dishonest with your spouse, e.g., by lying, gaslighting, cheating, or any form of deception, you show that you do not respect your spouse and are willing to do whatever you feel like doing to keep your spouse in consistent pain. When you dishonor your spouse, you are shaming and embarrassing them, and they will no longer feel comfortable disclosing their private feelings to you. When you are consistently obnoxious toward and in constant conflict with your spouse, you are deliberately hurting them and the relationship.

- Discipline breakers

    Tendency to gossip

    Selfishness

    Envy, jealousy

Discipline breakers are behaviors that exhibit a pattern of inconsistency with no regard for displaying respectful restraint with one's words and actions. When spouses participate in gossip by sharing personal and private details about their spouse and relationship without their spouse's approval, they are each disrespecting the relationship. A spouse who displays selfishness is focused solely on how their feelings, thoughts, and actions affect themselves and not on how they impact their spouse. Selfishness promotes the belief that one partner's thoughts and feelings are more important than their spouse's, and typically, the spouse's thoughts, ideas, and emotions are rejected, dismissed, or avoided. When this happens, your spouse's welfare is not your priority.

A partner who is jealous of another couple's relationship or their own spouse is generally not happy with themselves, focusing instead on criticizing their spouse, downgrading their spouse's achievements, and consistently making their partner feel as if they will never be enough in the relationship.

- Atmosphere breakers

    Arrogance
    Anger
    Resentment

Atmosphere breakers consist of emotions and actions that create an environment of hurt, pain, and condescension in the relationship.

When one partner continually exhibits arrogance and a strong sense of superiority over the other partner, this may create an unhealthy parent/child dynamic between the couple. Typically, when the parent/child dynamic is present, tension and fear are present as well. The partner in the "child" role usually feels taken for granted and that their thoughts and feelings do not matter in the relationship. Typically, they try to keep the peace to prevent conflict, and the partner in the "parent" role is usually responsible for causing this dynamic through fear, threats, and consequences. This type of atmosphere is very unhealthy for the relationship.

Whether one or both partners in the relationship are guilty of it, unresolved and toxic anger promotes fear and consistent panic because no one is listening or communicating in an emotionally safe manner. Typically, rage, screaming, blaming, and ignoring are common occurrences, and consequently, neither partner's opinions or feelings are heard because the pain and degradation makes it seem impossible to find a solution. Hence, an atmosphere of constant turmoil is created within the relationship.

Partners who are unwilling to forgive have suppressed anger that eventually turns into resentment and bitterness if the emotion is not handled in a healthy manner. Suppressed anger hurts the relationship because instead of releasing hurt and pain, it is constantly building up while simultaneously being ignored and avoided. This build-up of resentment creates an atmosphere of intense suffering in the relationship, both internally and externally.

Were you able to identify some of the marriage breakers present in your relationship? If so, consider how these marriage breakers impact your relationship.

When you practice disrespectful and destructive attributes, you show a lack of discipline, which creates an atmosphere of chaos in the relationship.

So, what can an individual do to stop these marriage breakers, and how can you and your partner show up in a healthy manner for your relationship? How does this relate to *your* relationship? What steps will you take to remove the breakers from your life and relationship?

CHAPTER 5

MARRIAGE BUILDERS

Building a successful relationship requires a continuous flow of peace and harmony. In this chapter, I will discuss marriage builders that can help you create your own safe space within your marriage relationship.

For a relationship to become healthy, it must be rebuilt through a different perspective by both partners in the relationship. A builder is an action that uplifts, encourages progress, focuses on the future, looks for solutions, and compromises. Likewise, listening to, uplifting, and supporting your partner is important for strengthening your relationship.

For a relationship to remain healthy, underlying issues must be discussed and dealt with. As issues are brought up, discussions begin to fill the gaps within the relationship, countering conflict with clarity and understanding about each other's perspectives to reach a productive and constructive outcome. Enlisting a third party—for example, a licensed professional who specializes in relationships—to assist in discussing problem areas is highly recommended.

Marriage Builder Attributes

The following attributes are marriage builders that can assist partners with sustaining the flow of power in the relationship to make it healthy and prosperous. The related questions will assess where you are presently in your relationship.

- Love – Do you have the ability to be unassuming, humble, respectful, patient, forgiving, positive, admiring, and perpetually truthful and honest with your partner, and look toward the future despite unhappy circumstances?

- Joy – Do you have an inner feeling of good cheer—comfort, optimism, and confidence—that you can pull from to alleviate feelings of discontent and misery that may arise in your relationship?

- Peace – Is your relationship generally free from disturbance? Do you experience periods in your relationship either free from conflict or marked by only brief conflicts with clear solutions?

- Patience – Do you have the capacity to accept or tolerate delay, trouble, or suffering within your relationship without getting angry or upset?

- Kindness – Are you considerate and supportive of your partner?

- Generosity – Are you unselfish, welcoming, free-giving, and hospitable with your partner, as well as emotionally pleasant even during unpleasant conversations?

- Faithfulness – Are you perpetually steadfast, loyal, consistent, and devoted to your partner?

- Gentleness – Do you maintain a calm and tender temperament without harshness with your partner, especially in conflict?

- Self-control – Do you purposely manage your own emotions, desires, and behaviors, particularly in difficult situations in your relationship?

The answers to these questions can help identify your weaknesses and strengths within the relationship.

Marriage Builder Categories

Marriage builders can be divided into three categories.

- Action builders

    Kindness

    Generosity

    Gentleness

Action builders are actions and activities that are purposely completed to ensure a particular result or conclusion. Kindness, generosity, and gentleness are important action builders that help create a safe emotional space for your spouse to become transparent with you and trust you again.

What are some actions rooted in kindness that you can do to support your spouse? What about doing household chores that your spouse despises, giving them a genuine compliment, giving your spouse all of your attention, listening to them converse about their day without criticisms, or listening to their frustrations without giving advice? Depending on your marital relationship, practicing kindness may involve doing something else, but the main idea is to be sure you do something kind for your spouse daily.

Generosity applies to more than just physical gifts. What are some things, you can do that will make your spouse feel special? For example, in emotional moments with your partner, are you comforting or harsh? Even if you are uncomfortable with emotions, being generous with your spouse ensures that they know that they are number one above everyone else in your life. The generous actions that you show your partner will help them feel that they are not competing with anyone for your love and attention and that you are truly present for them and the marriage relationship.

When you practice gentleness with your spouse, you are creating a safe space in which they can be transparent with their thoughts and feelings and showing them that their emotions matter to you. Gentleness means focusing on ensuring that your spouse feels heard. Your focus is not on waiting for them to finish speaking just to get your point across to them. Your focus is on continuing transparency, so engaging in a healthy manner is safe for both partners.

- Discipline builders

  Faithfulness

  Self-control

  Patience

Discipline builders are perpetual and habitual actions that create longevity and security which leads to a successful outcome. Faithfulness, patience, and self-control are crucial to create health and longevity for success and satisfaction in a marriage relationship.

Faithfulness in your relationship is a choice—a decision to be solely devoted to your partner, exhibiting loyalty and consistency in your speech and actions. When you do something wrong, apologize with both words and changed behavior. When you are angry with your partner, make the time and space to discuss your grievances and reach a resolution or compromise. When you have confirmed to them that you will do something or show up for something, follow through. If you are unable to honor your word, make contact beforehand, acknowledging the mishap with plans to correct it. Faithfulness in your relationship not only involves fidelity, but also consistency and ensuring your word is your bond.

When your partner can trust your word, the trust level in other areas in the relationship increases.

Self-control in a relationship involves understanding that inappropriate and toxic behavior will not be tolerated without consequences. Types of inappropriate and toxic behavior can include verbal, emotional, psychological, physical, and financial abuse. When a partner or couple engages in these behaviors, lack of self-control turns into trying to control their partner. When a partner is unable to control their own emotions and focuses on controlling their partner, an unsafe environment is created, stunting the growth of the relationship. As a result, healthy expectations and communication within the relationship slowly begin to break down.

In a relationship, patience is a key ingredient of discipline. A partner who is patient with his or her spouse has made the decision to tolerate their spouse's positive and negative emotions in a positive manner, with the goal of creating a safe space for direct and honest communication. By practicing patience with your spouse, you are indirectly stating that they can come to you regardless of the situation because you have decided to be present for your partner in their time of need.

- Atmosphere builders

  Love
  Joy
  Peace

Atmosphere builders are activities and actions that promote a continual environment of harmony and health in the well-being of both partners. Love, joy, and peace are significant atmosphere builders in a relationship because they create a secure emotional space for spouses to communicate about uncomfortable and conflicting topics.

Love is an amazing element in a relationship. When love is present, and a couple's thoughts, feelings, and actions are aligned, satisfaction in the relationship is greatly increased. Love is not a fleeting emotion—it is a decision. When a partner tells their spouse, "I love you," it should be because the partner has decided that they are ready to forgive, and be humble, respectful, truthful, honest, and positive about the past, present and future despite any unhappy circumstances the relationship may endure.

Where there is joy, there is unending happiness. A relationship that has joy declares that the couple is on an ongoing path toward pleasing one another while also balancing their self-care. Joy allows the couple to focus on being productive in the relationship and place the emphasis on the best and healthy parts of the relationship, even when facing challenging situations.

Peace is achieved when a couple decides that even when they may have conflicts, they will view these conflicting moments as growing experiences and a part of learning about each other and improving the relationship. The decision to choose peace is reaffirmed every day throughout the couple's relationship. Each partner chooses to speak peace, think peace, and act peaceably with one another. In every circumstance, whether in a social, political, or work environment, each partner has decided to strive for peace in all areas in their lives. When partners focus on planting seeds of peace, the resulting crop grows, nourishes, and provides a harmonious environment for the relationship. Choosing peace is choosing light and life in the furtherance of the relationship.

How can these marriage builder attributes be applied to your marriage to construct a healthy marriage relationship?

You must create the atmosphere that you want in your life and in your marriage relationship through discipline. Ultimately, you must act with kindness, generosity, and gentleness while practicing self-control, faithfulness, and patience if you desire to create an atmosphere of love, joy, and peace in your relationship.

Are you ready to implement marriage builders to improve your marriage relationship? What specific steps will you take?

CHAPTER 6
RELATIONSHIP SECURITY SYSTEM

Securing your marital relationship is a vital part of striving for a healthy relationship. This chapter will identify a relationship security system (RSS) that will assist you in maintaining the marriage builders discussed in the previous chapter.

What is a relationship security system? An RSS is a system for protecting the relationship from harm, securing the relationship from threats and danger, and keeping the relationship emotionally and physically safe from internal factors, external factors, and marriage breakers that can obstruct peace in the relationship.

Is your relationship protected from both external and internal factors? External factors may include family, friends, work, drugs, and other extracurricular activities that may prevent you from spending quality time with your partner. These external factors, along with many others, can intrude on the relationship. Internal factors can include grudges you hold against your partner, negative emotions about your partner that you have not communicated yet, and secrecy. Internal factors can intrude and hinder the growth of a relationship. Ultimately, successful relationships must have protection, security, and safety from external elements, internal elements, and marriage breakers.

KEY RSS ELEMENTS

- Protection – How do you prevent your spouse or your marital relationship from suffering emotional, physical, and mental harm?

- Security – Do you provide the space for your spouse and marital relationship to be free from emotional, mental, and physical danger?

- Safety – How do you defend and shield your spouse and marital relationship from exposure to physical, mental, and emotional threats/risks?

RSS THREATS

- Emotional harm or danger – A strong emotional reaction, such as embarrassment, humiliation, degradation, shame, or dishonor caused indirectly or directly by another person

- Mental harm/injury/danger – Consistent verbal abuse or assault, such as cursing, name calling, coercion, manipulation, intimidation, bullying, and constant criticism

- Physical harm/injury/danger – Direct bodily injury, or the potential of physical injury caused by another

Every relationship has some form of an RSS. Determining whether your system is a strong or weak one is essential. Typically, how you and your partner handle conflicts can show you which category your RSS falls into.

If your RSS is weak, what has prevented it from becoming solid? What behaviors must you stop for your system to be strong? What factors continue to infiltrate your system? What steps will you take to ensure that your RSS is working effectively?

CONCLUSION

I am positive that you certainly do *not* want to experience either an "accidental" or intentional divorce! And by applying the tools, tips, and strategies described in this book, you won't have to. You can actually create and sustain a joyful and peaceful marriage relationship with your partner.

The major determining factor to its success is the work that you and your partner are willing to do to contribute to the relationship. Self-assessment can clarify your own self-development, which in turn can help you determine which strategies to follow with your spouse. Understanding what healthy versus unhealthy marital relationships look like can help you recognize which level your relationship presently resides in.

In addition, assessing your relationship can identify attributes that you may want to consider developing as you work on creating a healthy relationship. Learning about marriage breakers can help you identify attributes and actions that you and your partner may need to cease in order to create a peaceful environment for your relationship. Understanding the importance and benefits of marriage builders can strengthen your hope and increase your desire to change negative behaviors as you strive for greater joy in the marital relationship.

Finally, by examining and strengthening your relationship security system, you and your partner can unleash the power to transform the relationship into the marital paradise that you both desire to live your lives in together.

■ ■ ■

www.ingramcontent.com/pod-product-compliance
Lightning Source LLC
Chambersburg PA
CBHW050919160426
43194CB00011B/2471